THIS BOOK BELONGS TO:

_____

The material on this book is copyrighted and belongs to Mapogo Publishing and Antonio Arredondo. 2021.

CARNOTAURUS SASTREI

A CARNIVORE MEMBER OF THE "ABELISAURIDAE" FAMILY, HIS NAME MEANS "MEAT EATING BULL", IS BELIEVED THAT THIS DINOSAUR WAS ONE OF THE FASTEST PREDATORS.

ANKYLOSAURUS

AN ARMOURED HERVIBORE, THIS DINOSAUR USED THE CLUB ON IT`S TAIL TO FIGHT BIG PREDATORS.

OVIRAPTOR

IT`S NAME MEANS "EGG THIEF" THIS DINOSAUR LIVED AROUND 75 MILLION YEARS AGO, ON WHAT ASIA IS TODAY.

TRICERATOPS

HIS NAME MEANS "FACE WITH THREE HORNS" IS THE MOST FAMOUS MEMBER OF THE CERATOPSIAN FAMILY, AND IS ALSO THE MOST FAMOUS ENEMY OF THE T-REX.

PTERODACTYL

THIS ANIMAL IS NOT ACTUALLY A DINOSAUR, BUT A FLYING REPTILE

TYRANNOSAURUS REX V.S. TRICERATOPS

ONE OF THE MOST FAMOUS SCENES OF PREHISTORIC TIMES, IS THE FIGHT BETWEEN THE KING OF LIZARDS AND THE POWERFUL HEVIBORE, DEPICTED IN MANY MOVIES AND BOOKS.

DEINONYCHUS ANTIRRHOPUS

A VICIOUS HUNTER, TRAVELED IN PACKS AND HAD A SHARP CLAW ON THEIR FEET.

PROTOCERATOPS

ANOTHER MEMBER OF THE CERATOPCIAN FAMILY, HIS NAME RELATES TO AN ANCIENT FACE WITH HORNS OR "FIRST FACE WITH HORNS", HE IS FAMOUSLY, AN ADVERSARY OF THE VELOCIRAPTOR

TYRANNOSAURUS REX

THE MOST FAMOUS DINOSAUR, RECENT FINDINGS SUGGEST THAT THIS DINOSAUR HAD FEATHERS

APATOSAURUS

A SAUROPOD DINOSAUR, LIVED DURING THE JURASSIC PERIOD AND HAD A LONG NECK TO REACH HIGH BRANCHES AND TREES.

GORGOSAURUS LIBRATUS

A TYRANNOSAURID, A SMALLER VERSION OF HIS COUSIN, THE T-REX.

CARNOTAURUS

A MEMBER OF THE ABELISAURID FAMILY, ITS ARMS WERE SO TINY THAT THEY WERE VESTIGIAL AND PRACTICALLY USELESS

STEGOSAURUS

ANOTHER FAMOUS DINOSAUR, IS SAID THAT HIS BRAIN WAS SMALLER THAN A CHESTNUT. THE SPIKES ON HIS TAIL WAS NAMED "THAGOMIZER"

CERATOSAURUS NASICORNIS

HIS NAME MEANS "LIZARD WITH A HORN ON THE NOSE"

PARASAUROLOPHUS

HAD A BIG CREST ON HIS HEAD AND TRAVELED ON HEARDS, WAS A LARGE HADROSAURUS

SPINOSAURUS

ONE OF THE DINOSAURS WITH MORE CHANGES OVER THE YEARS, HE RECEIVES HIS NAME FROM THE SAIL-LIKE SPINE ON HIS BACK.

ALLOSAURUS FRAGILIS

A LARGE AND FIERCE PREDATOR, THIS DINOSAUR LIVED DURING THE FINAL STAGES OF THE JURASSIC PERIOD

PACHYCEPHALOSAURUS

HIS NAME MEANS "LIZARD WITH A THICK HEAD" IS BELIEVED THEY USED THEIR HEADS TO CLASH WITH ONE ANOTHER, MUCH LIKE MODERN RAMS DO TODAY

BRACHIOSAURUS

ONE OF THE LARGEST HERVIBORES, TRAVELED IN HEARDS AND WAS SO BIG THAT PROBABLY, NO PREDATOR DARED TO HUNT HIM, OR THEY RISKED BEING STUMPED ON

DILOPHOSAURUS WETHERILLI

ANOTHER DINOSAUR THAT HAD CHANGES OVER THE YEARS, WAS A FIERCE PREDATOR EVEN WHEN THERE IS NO PROOF THAT HIS SALIVA WAS VENOMOUS, AS PEOPLE THINK BECAUSE OF A FAMOUS DINOSAUR MOVIE

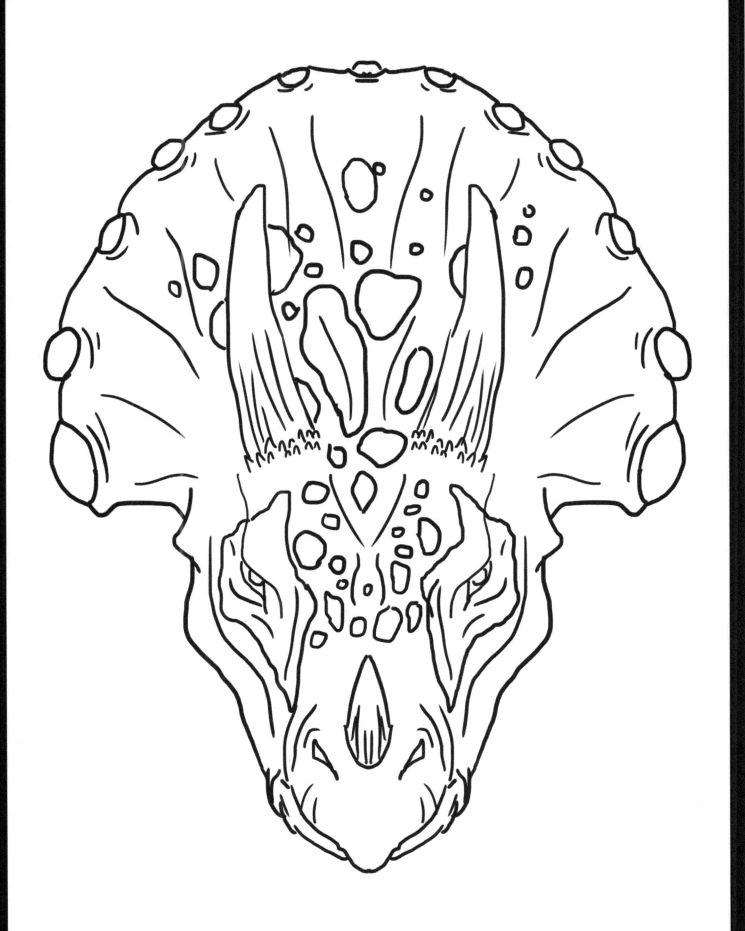

TRICERATOPS HEAD

A FIERCE LOOK FROM ONE OF THE WILDEST PREDATORS

VELOCIRAPTOR

A PACK HUNTER THAT IS NOW BELIEVED TO BE COVERED ON FEATHERS, HE WAS ALSO NOT AS BIG AS IN THE MOVIES, BEING AROUND THE SIZE OF A LARGE TURKEY

PLESIOSAUR

A LONG NECK AQUATIC REPTILE

UTAHRAPTOR

THE LARGEST MEMBER OF THE DROMEOSAURID FAMILY, IS "THE THIEF OF UTAH" A BIG RAPTOR WITH A FIERCE INSTINCT

ALBERTACERATOPS

A CERATOPSIAN FOUND IN ALBERTA CANADA, HENCE HIS NAME.

BABY DINOSAUR

IS BELIEVED THAT MOTHER DINOSAURS TOOK CARE OF THEIR NESTS FOR REASONABLE PERIOD OF TIME

GALLIMIMUS BULLATUS

LIGHT FRAME AND LONG LEGS, THIS DINOSAUR WAS MADE TO RUN... FAST

BRACHIOSAURUS

ONE OF THE LARGEST DINOSAURS, HE COULD WEIGHT OVER 39 TONS

iGUANODON

ANOTHER LARGE HADROSAUR, HAD SPIKES ON THE FRONT HANDS THAT HE USED TO DEFEND HIMSELF.

MICROCERATOPS

THE SMALLEST CERATOPSIAN